sticky notes

indy yelich

sticky notes

indy yelich

www.indyyelich.com

Cover photography by Sophia Doak. About Author
Image by Will Tee Yang.
Back Cover Illustration by Greta Markurt.

sticky notes
indy yelich

for sonja yelich,
'in ways i am a mirror of you.'

LA

thievery
as if all i read is my horoscope
delicate us
my only company is the sunset
beach of my abandoned body parts
my sofa
friends of the escapade
ode to a sour day
flamingo
boulders
curse of the meat-sweat hands
bow
living in la
saudade
scarletina
unintended spring
bird feet
untitled.
satan is cellular
angel town
hero
forget me not
grocery store hell
if only i spoke swedish
mediocre & such
the ing
chateau marmont
wrong colour to be feeling so young

NY

2nd avenue
cheater plants
the middle of a soho party, 9.59pm
bask
bucket full of snakes
maybe i just need glasses
i smell my beach-house on macdougal st, nyc
central park
strings
guest list
bottomless drip-time coffee
molly ringwald's prom dress
trees have great manners
harvest hungry
dish cloth
a day in west harlem
bleeding french tip manicure
biscuits
falling in fall
ivy cafe
bs to the bs to the bs
fickle friendship club
halloween night
ny-sea
a bridge into the city
nerves in november
goodwill
ember chest
sticky notes
a cheeto runs the world
the coincidence of livy
potion
to be a year older in new york
penny for your sight

LA

thievery

comparison is the thief of joy
my worst enemy
  the one
who at 4am
sneaks into the apartment
and steals my breath

he makes the weather   in my mind
muggy
not because it's 95 degrees outside
the summer solstice

he carries knives
sharpened with a rock
he keeps lodged
under my ribs

please, thief! not today

but moving over my back
he whispers adamantly
into my   seashell ears

who will you ever be

    nobody
        nothing

give up
    stop
you'll only ever be the sister

as if all i read is my horoscope

in this day
and in this age

everybody seems to be angry
or hungry.

the covfefe orange
is too outspoken

it's offensive if you're not a feminist
it's offensive if you are one

i whisper quietly my political status to no one in particular
a small cartoon of words

about anything really serious -

white noise is an opinion
i need more education
my acting coach says

i la times
i Whitney
i lacma

& i know how it feels to be shamed for wearing shorts

delicate us

i have to accept
that our natural language
didn't include words

silently
soaking in your honey sweat skin
limb-grazing in a velvet sea
laughing about the encyclopaedias
stacked in your wardrobe

       the kitchen bench
in the storm
arms wrapped up in neck
  soft rain speaks of us

and now
i'm on the International Voyage of finding myself
leaving you for
the other side of the ocean
& aeroplanes

the clock is a prison sentence
all i have left are the memories
that haunt me
in my shower

crosslegged
eating cereal

wondering why it tastes
so off

my only company is the sunset

pink reaches for my ponytail and pulls
hair escapes, silky & almost dry
pink jumps off my balcony
into the sky
how did she do that!
she's found a lover,
blue.
and you can feel the purple of
their lovemaking
merging as one
as lovers should
but yellow
yellow stays high
to the right of me,
maybe he is scared because
i haven't seen him in a few days
he hides behind trees i do not know
the names of
there he'll stay until pink has finished with blue
and they have gone home.
and i will be stuck, waiting for their return.

beach of my abandoned body parts

take my willow soul
put it in a jar
hurl it in the waves

my sofa

my sofa must think i'm a little weird
because i'm a sea urchin
a lousy hermit crab
       bitter sharp pincers
moping about the apartment with a
messy brain

i wonder what my sofa would say if it
could speak
really? existential thoughts at 18?
why are you so pensive
if you're not even living
you're just in a living room

you don't have it rough
all i get for company are teenage arses

friends of the escapade

my life was the thrilling blue flame
a lecturing parent couldn't match my lionheart
in other words, the pied piper of sneaking out
tiptoed along bleached oak
past my surrogate grandfather's garage light
beaming,
me,
tail-lighted.

but my parents didn't stir
and oh, i would live
   for those nights
sneaking down to the beach
ten of the shiniest people
trading innocent kisses with a boy
 fifteen year old eyes looked up
at the sky so light
and i knew.
i was all seeing.
or so my coral brain perceived

lilac   sea air
nectar of smirnoffs
crushed up behind my bookshelves
equivalent to empty beef jerky packets

boys climbed through thorn and worm
to tap on my window
only to be ushered away by my mother's
bathroom light

every night
the boisterous tui
or cat door
would almost give me away
as i crept,
child night jungle
full moon's parental glare

inside me grew things
words spoken
(that could never be uttered in the shy-day)
brushing of hands
lips on necks

the night-time land of my 15s.

ode to a sour day

we sunbathe so i don't go off
the deep
end

the socials   erased from my phone as
        nothing is more angering than
    i wish i had known him better

a friend brings me tropical tea with mint
i even have a baby spoon

a stuffed crocodile is my softest limb now
tear ducts are rusty taps
dripping
at your category of RIP

        but today   they are off
        everything's off
        the sky is my sunken cheek

flamingo

there is only so much you can do,
to mould.
to shape, to wax, to cut curves.
silencing your opinion is not always
elegant
sometimes it just makes you sound
stupid.
we (the better parts of me)
pity you

for letting you wobble on one foot
are you a flamingo
don't be so pink

say
something.

what's the point
i'll just be shouting into the void

but voices
voices weren't shaped
to sound a certain way
words don't resonate
carefully clipped around the edges

boulders

get out of the way *lovers*
 as the morning   seeps

around me

dull
a flat sea

i won't collect sea shells
i don't care for touching hands
i don't want to share

          boulders are my complacent heart

i do not love
you've stolen that

curse of the meat-sweat hands

recently
i've been held by
no-one   in particular
flinching when they touch me
or jump out   pretending

i see holes in walls
blood-knuckles
        like my father's zinnias
are you gonna push me

apologies to your first bike
yanked off training wheels
rusting in the backyard

purple doesn't suit my arms
and knees
but   would look great on a t-shirt

bow

i thought that going out dancing would be grando
but i woke up lonelier than ever
lugging my laptop to the bourgeois pig

it feels like sunday
because of the lazy
air around me
and such

  lou's telling me to just do it
take a walk on the wild side!
but i'm not exactly sure how to
things don't fall together unless you
superglue them

my creativity has gone   walk a bouts
i feel it resting on my shoulders but
it's been too black to see properly
in cafes, bowed heads on hands don't always mean
sorrow
but lethargic dreams

living in la

yesterday i was standing in this bar
called delilah
with gypsy

and i was trying not to let the brain cells
slip out of my head
and stain the pavement

listening to instagram conversation about
her lips being fake
and drake was about to pull up
breasts were pushed up
hair slicked back
and my eyes rolled back
so far
i thought i'd have to dive into my head and retrieve them.

saudade

the real tragedy
isn't the nighttime
when you're alone
with uncomfortable pillows

it's the hum of reminder
that there are no extra hands
so you hold yourself in the dark
the bleak self-caress

(hunger for the touch
passion stolen from the passionate)

i am the lost and found pile
grubby hands rummage through
the discarded

i kiss for the body
to steal the warmth
    ignoring the human attached

the love that remains
leaks out of my fingers
lost in the 99c bananas

scarletina

i ache to write the way people want
but i can't
i am the velveteen rabbit
through each word
maybe i become

real

unintended spring

nights last until 2am
scouring for more time

until i have conquered
   alexander the great

starred
  out   the   sky
the sister is an identity

so deep-rooted
  bark is growing
on my wrists
     spreading up my arms

sap pours out of my ears so
i can't hear my own name
being called

see how vivid yellow goes grey

bird feet

as i lay numb
reach out and touch me with sunshine rays
let me hear your laughter in a whistling bird
make the ocean kiss my ankles

so i am invited in
no running and squealing in your house

you could not be free in your body

but i hear bird feet in the grass
i see fresh lemons swelling

for you are not gone
i see you in every sunrise

untitled.

snowstorm tainted with blood
ivy that crawls up the house in albert park
plug in a mower and cause havoc
i know you can

i see flecks of you
everywhere i go
freckles of your psyche are found in stranger's
eyes&cheeks
outside duane reade

in passing.

and streets like franklin village
san vincente

how you hurt the ones you love
i will never understand

satan is cellular

blackberries on the table
brought by my mother

she mumbled something
about going to the
farmers market
while i numb out
on my cellphone

look up
i yell at yesterday's fool

angel town

fishnets
pumped up gas station fishy mouths
artificial sun
many moons in the day time
aka gleaming porcelain teeth
ripped up band tees
90s sunglasses
french bulldogs named Sam or Paris
brushing past me
while i search for trinkets
for my junk room
at the Melrose Trading Post.

my mind cuts into people's appearances
anything to avoid me
messy me
big thighed, sleepy eyed me.
pimples near forehead
swollen lips
REAL FRIENDS
i can count on one hand.
and a mind running about the centuries
searching for things that cannot be found
here in this angel town.

hero

you have oval fingernails that change colour when school
is out
weird-o disjointed thumbs
i think you were placed in the wrong era
because you don't go outside and you eat books
like sandwiches
your hair hangs wet
i can smell coconut & i am hazed
your mechanics need to be oiled and i try
bleeding out adoration so that you can function
you are yellow flowers in a forgotten field
i tell you i want us to go to Pompeii because ancient
history
takes us somewhere
        with fresh air

i lean my head on your lap everyday before school 'cause
i'm weak
and you are here

your vinyl spins round & round when we lie on your
quilted sheet
i'm careful not to spill coffee on it
black and white frames are pinned on your bedroom wall
of the girls that Hero You Up.
feeding me popcorn and
    pretending to love me
you tie me to the park bench and hide a wrench
from your father's garden toolshed
        behind your back
beating my nose in so my lungs spill out

when you were surprised with an oak cello   you wept
and i weep
now

forget me not

because of you,
it's august
come to me sunshine!
let the forget-me-knots grow
should i brew a potion
to awaken
my becoming september
heart

grocery store hell

it's a trek down la cienaga with paris
we've been doing everyday for two weeks
it's a trek to get to the bank of america
to deposit rent all in twenties

it's not the coral singlet
   tucked
into my denim skirt
that gets them going

paris wears a prairie girl top & sheer white sleeves
the vision of *whatever pure is*
honks   words   men
fat eyes cutting into my
   nipples
looking out through
my singlet

a little down the street
we are asked for photos
probably for his wank bank
a Feral calls out from his car   *mami!*
 as if he could ever touch me

kiwis   eye-fucked galore
and we are taught
to cover up
for fear of a pervert who cannot help himself

just let us walk in the daytime
without fear of being assaulted

if only i spoke swedish

now she is gone & i'm cloroxing my house
the white chairs are scrubbed good
i know you don't say good like that

madness is an ikea apartment

stained catalina market mugs lie about
and sick of loading the dishwasher alone
they are accidentally
smashed in the sink
(like my lukewarm dreams)

skyy, malibu, svedka &
chateau marmont wine beckon

but i don't have the stomach for them

mediocre & such

happy
but perusing
there's a shortness
of breath

when i talk about my
 fleeting youth

                    and i still

let myself
dream the hours away

sweating
and
 running

 brain treadmills
at night

around the ceilings
up the walls
    through the mini kitchen

only to find that there
is nothing to prove
to anyone
but the disappointed
ghost inside my
ribcage

the ing

meanwhile
my skull is nagging me

she wants to hear rain sounds on a tin roof
she doesn't really like sirens and obnoxious garages
opening at 5am
but she couldn't be anywhere else at 18
amongst the salmon skies

recalling the lilac lady on the vma stage
her truth is a-banging

       through a boombox and a disco tinsel 15-y/o dress

and if it weren't for the lilac lady

my skull would be rattling about in a ferry building
waiting for a 9am lecture

chateau marmont

behold
los angeles *vivacity*
midnight neon noise
that i can taste
all down
my throat

sienna
cayenne red
plum
the colours race
past my fingernails

you can hear people
loving
for all of the night
knees under my dress
to fight the cold

but outside
all my windows
there is only west hollywood
at its finest

    i do not miss you anymore
    but maybe your hands
    just a little

wrong colour to be feeling so young

as i wash off the day
she's living inside me

i eat for two people
i write for two people

blue so thick   bile is rising
so i tell my mom i need
help

after four years
i admit

i just know i can't use my friends
as therapists!

its the
    taint
the black ink   shroud
  standards i set
for myself

i wonder how i lived through high school
i wonder how i never worried about moving
to a different continent
only   worrying how long i could stay

self-hades
get your blades away from me!

it wasn't until 12.37 am that
it hit me
i'm unwell
this isn't what 18
 should feel like

NY

2nd avenue

so many likes so little love
stickered to a yellow parking meter
trash cans jammed full
spines and corduroy pants
trotting past the pavement
fire escapes that edward climbed up
to save vivian
even though she said she didn't need saving
and he was afraid of heights
she wasn't just a pretty woman.

i love the blatancy of this town
gardens flourish from the tops of
12 storey buildings
likewise, i grow high up
    the coat of dirt that blankets
The Whole of New York
gives it a
don't fuck with me touch
& a, but love me anyway!

what is this eeriness?
the one that enters without knocking
into my spaghetti of a brain.
the uncertainty
about all of this
clacking of feet that won't commit
to a job and a university.
To anyone really.

when will i find my in-between?

cheater plants

the weeds crept and grew
      nearing the rose bush

i begged the weeds to stop
but they wouldn't listen

and the drought that followed

after a few months, rain appeared
sobbing over the plants
wishing to bring them
life once more

but they were dead
and

there was nothing anybody could do
not even the most exquisite gardener

the middle of a soho party, 9.59pm

i miss your
honeycomb voice

bask

when i'm grown
i do not want
demure
grey-meek
because of a failed lover.
i want
wilted limbs
speckled hands
crows feet
the lot!
crinkle-eye laughing
on a sunday
even in drippy sad weather
thank god, there's no soccer game today
and the kids are staying at my sister's house
and we get to sleep in until 10am
old and basking in it
like my parents

bucket full of snakes

let it fill you with dread
let the clouds come weeping
pleading with you to stay
let the snakes curl around your organs
while you wait for the end
but is it the end?

when you haven't given your words
to the world
    you can pack It all
into 1 suitcase
& find home within

if the crowds aren't hyena-calling out
your name

why let them take

                        you

            tame

don't let your haemoglobin run cold
just yet

maybe i just need glasses

the day was drunk
and my stupid leaking heart
told you to come lie down with me

you are the poison
when i stop drinking
i hope i will see clearly again

i smell my beach-house on macdougal st, nyc

amongst sand   flowery dinner plates
my family
debate who caught the biggest fish

and i'm the yellow walls
lapsed in love and seashell smell

all the times i milled about home
anti beach house
loner lazy with a pool and boyfriend

and now
i would pay
in time tokens
to be back
around vic & sonja
ella & jerry
and little angelo

bickering about whose gonna do the dishes

growing up is too complex   you want
back
what you shook your head at
when you were young

central park

i just want to
sit in the park
a little while longer

strings

the catastrophe -
is that you saw me
in the rain when we were locked out of the house

i didn't feel like the daughter i could have been
and i wept through your love
like a sieve
a square with no fucking sides
emptying out

we would take walks
outside the auckland war museum
  as i wanted
  to be   by the
      dew

you were given a key
not just to my house
but to my sister's smile
mama's cooking
my father's straw hat
little angel angelo's skepticism about growing older

her name lit up your screen
and i was confused

when love notes   polaroids   texts   were so pungent
with guilt

your parents split
so you split me &
the world

i exclaim in disdain
you -
through the ripples of black
cutting me.
i will have to see a therapist for $400 an hour
thanks for unwinding all the strings!

guest list

the way you made me feel
is similar to when someone says

 'what party?'

(their voice in their feet)

the feeling you shared with somebody else
that i wasn't invited to

but

it was my 18th
   i bought the streamers.

bottomless drip-time coffee

time is the currency
alone in my studio in west harlem

    the world whirs

my fridge breathes
keeping the food cold

i am rich on a saturday morning
but sunday night forget it

a day of errands turn into a week

i fight between satisfaction & an itch
to be a teenager
or a conquerer

my 12pm apt
feels like 2am.
no light,
& so, i sleep
a little longer

molly ringwald's prom dress

where is your head? they ask
oh god i wish i could tell you

somewhere near the beat generation
on molly ringwald's bed as she makes her prom dress
all pink
wrapped around bukowski's words

part of the snow
that reminds me of bon iver

a child lulled, resting in a daisy field
as father and son is strummed by cat stevens

swirling around van gogh's stars
    the cobbled stoned rues of 1920s paris

the entrance to mount olympus.

in love with all things made up
in between centuries
lost
  dead
yearning.

trees have great manners

walking around manhattan is like drinking coffee
    the sweet rush
even though i've been caffeine free for six months
i still miss it

it's hard to imagine
you tucked up
in your striped blue sheets
snoring
lonely

you can't see my
red paint lips

eating starbucks banana bread
 legs too short for chair

and you can't see the central park trees
bending softly in the wind

    they're bowing for me

i go to tell you about all of this
  and the trees
    whisper seasons
     in my ear

disapproving

harvest hungry

you made me love you!
i exclaim,
    the toddler

finger pointed
neck bent low
fear burrowing

you let us rise & fall
& when my hands met
your skin
i knew that i was doomed

what will become of me;
ode to the moth
on the outside of the glass
begging for the light

dish cloth

thinking of a new york autumn
i am laced with the memory of   the yellow submarine
dish cloth green leaves
on the neighbouring trees in Central Park

i see a man sitting under an almost tree
a king charles pup in lap
he could be the most evil man in the world
but that dog is loveable

i'm so focused on the future
i can't eat up the present
and the mothers and their children
in the strollers

girl in a fleecy red coat
          behind a lamppost
little boy sits next to me   in the cold

inquisitive eyes & denim
where is your mother

this is the time for the cherub children
who make me forget

     all the eyes taking in the leaves for the first time

this park is designed for a crisp 4 o'clock.
for nannies and infants
for people getting from place to place but
taking their sweet time about it.

a day in west harlem

scrub out side street grime
stinking subway heat
& i've got west harlem

i walk down 125th st
a block away from where i live
hands full of vegetables & clorox
because i just dyed my hair black

and there's the townhouse church with the red door
a wizened woman stops me
to talk about birds
chattering in the church tree

i pass the bakery pie
lamb chop smell
halal cart

on the corner of duane reade
(i enter for an m&m snack)
a man sells cds
music blasting from a no bullshit stereo
none of that ue boom beat

harlem and the east village probably wouldn't get along
but both have threadbare people & snobs

i don't know if it's the baby smiling at me   despite the
surly mother
 that makes me feel like there is sun
inside my heart
or that i just returned from the moma

but beauty is heavy thick
hiding under grass
in dilapidated buildings
on st nicholas ave

bleeding french tip manicure

be thirsty
for the knowledge
that sits on the bookshelf

pleading

rise from the scrolling slumber
and see   your thumbs   the buildings that walk past you

get into the dirt
digging so deep
your manicured fingers   bleed

if you let the hot cyber state infest your mind
you will go shallow
there will be no wading

i could have bought a better life at target

words are attached
to my liver
    the depths that shake
    the qualms
        the palms that shiver

sitting sponge-like indoors
will
    kill
        the hunger

biscuits

the peculiarity of pain
is that we only feel ours

i feel nothing
when you smell
the cologne
after many months.
those memories
this loss!

and we butt heads
(careless sheep)
trying to prove
our pain is
the most relevant

a rib-cracking laugh
crumbled in half
(shared like a biscuit)

your mother died today.
january 23rd.
and my s.o
march.
but those are just days
to everyone else

falling in fall

i've never seen
so much enthusiasm come from
a pack of gum
you offer your socks up
because my feet are blistered
(from walking to you!)

i've never known
someone's entire body to morph
into their own Jupiter
when they listen to songs that
make them feel alive
& yet, you're blue

i would faint and take up
sporadic
ballet classes
before i asked you out

so i sit
hollowed out in my room
full of maybe lights
could have been lights
staring at apartments that wave
through windows
& darken as people sleep
too afraid to take the chance

tonight
i am falling like the leaves that crunch
under my boots
as i traipse on home

ivy cafe

it's beautiful to be forgotten
in a city like this

pansies grow in a window box
outside La Lanterna Di Vittorio

    strength of rain
smell of cappuccinos

people-ants march on home

i want more than ever
to have a little studio
right by washington square
& i'll fill it with poetry
i've collected from the side street
book markets

you will call me to say   look outside
the window (the realist)

& there you are
grinning amongst the growling thunder

but it's the sunniest day i've ever seen in manhattan

bs to the bs to the bs

nyu couch
finds my body
most weekends
the one who really loves me.

tonight
  i translate
the unspoken french
of how much someone
can take from you

to suit themselves
must i balance on this trapeze

girls summon
  party tears
after alcohol
  their skinny love bullshit

& i watch

in one night
i: giver & taker

have seen whoever's controlling
this fucking *purple* universe
life breathe jealousy
& compassion
into my friends

(self love in teaspoons. tonight it's running down the
gutter)

hungry
 shaking
desperate
loveable

filled to the brim with crystal palace vodka

fickle friendship club

winter brings an epidemic
the garden where i work
    dies

my part-time lover has no more love to give
new yorkers become wasps
for subway seats
& the last hot chocolate

you sink smaller into your college dorm
sending shame brain waves
branding me
loud & inferior

the evening light
slotted for 8pm
darkens at 4:52

halloween night

teenage mutant ninja turtles
    little cats
witches
truck ramming into citibikers
     8 murdered

an eery mauve air calm
people walkie-talkie sidewalk cellphoning

could have been one of my nyu friends
but it's not.
after work, i take shelter on the brownstone steps
to breathe
to answer the calls

for the first time, i'm in the thick of it
3 streets away
ambulances
hours of
crying metal tears at the scene

    despite this,
we're all lovers over here.
      so many flowers in the east village
       macdougal street in petals

inside the bean normalcy resumes
the remedy
 is listening to people complain
mundane brings the colours
back.

ny-sea

midnight isolation
drips through wall
and ceiling

what are the urbanists (once suburban)
doing in their apts at 1:49am
who are they talking to
are they sitting crosslegged on the floor

remembering you
is like looking into a fog
and seeing a silhouette in the distance

you walk through my blood
with __ size shoes i can't recall
doing sprints along my toes
            to my bellybutton

new york is my only friend
her noisy arrogance
street car sirens
put on a show!
fortissimo

        time on a loop

a bridge into the city

horoscopes say the same thing
i think about the world in the bath
sky so miserable
new yorkers are crying before 5.30

this murky water
all these weird-ass hickeys on my shoulder

try be like jack gilbert or frank o'hara
with a touch of rupi kaur for relatabilty

but make it specific to you.
this is what they're telling me
some want cut fingers & tongues from picking
up my almost book
and inhaling the words

some say take your time
all i know is that
in this book
there's too much talk
about pretty drunk greasy illuminated boy
dreamy oak floors and brick walls

nerves in november

winged serpent
simplicity in the way that i love
      turned violent

iridescence of my insides
beating & nagging me for something

more

     too many locker room tears
award shows speaking truth
is this within my reach

she's stuck in the summer
    she's stuck in now and forever
she can't use the plastic forks
to cut open her heart

too many shiners
too many memories
that rub her the wrong way

will the scorpio season
calm the anxiety inside

goodwill

side-by-side we
lollop along bleecker st
following the crowd

& my eyes smile as i see the marks on your sweater
that you bought from a thrift store

we can't decide if it's egg white

                          but i could paint
 cream   the walls of my
house
    or just

                dirty yellow

                        and stare at them

forever

you like
the way i sing
& carve words
out of wooden past memories

i am the creaking of a door
do i creep along the floorboards
for fear of waking you up
or should i nudge you gently
and litter the room with my love

ember chest

you are wood
stacked
  in the fireplace of my stomach

sticky notes

spoon-fed media
we don't search. for anything.

categories
university
9-5
marriage
kids
picket fence. i don't want white, what about yellow?
or blue.

pulling at my thighs, wondering,
is this normal?
i can see a few rolls now.

of course it is.

3.52am: sticky notes on door, fridge, cupboard.
eat healthy.
do sit-ups.
take out trash.

i am so incapable
will i not remember?

dreaming of devonport.
and the new prime minister.
who believes in mental health awareness.
and that you have your own rights
as a woman

so full of knowledge. so full of doubt.
do you say 'so full' like this?

do you see colours the way i do?
will this pan out the way that i want?
is everything just a little easier at 3.55am?
why am i best friends with the darkness?

a cheeto runs the world

irked about the elephants
trump encourages to slaughter
with the new law

and now the fuckwit men are being
called out
for bringing their luncheon meat near us

i wanna hustle but also just sleep through the winter

the coincidence of livy

it's overwhelming to know
what i know
and not be able to discuss it.
there is no lock on my voice box

but a furrowed brow
grumpy critic
silence me.

so i sit on this mossy bench
full of it.
learning about the tragedy of sylvia plath
and all the greatest poets, who chose death
and my closest, chose death.

a squirrel with a nut
squeezes through the protruding wire
a gang of bully birds fly overhead
so close to my head i feel the breath of the wind
and a family of 4 are caught in this bird moment
laughing at the close proximity

a lazy park bench   guitar
dances past my ears

my oldest friend livy
strolls past in her nasa jacket
of all the people in the world
it's her!
she reminds me of ella
funny how you find parts of people in others

i'm coming to terms with not enough time now
as the tuba & sax blow my ear drums out my feet
under the washington square arch

potion

you can't trust me
i'll take your tears
            moonlight words
& mix them in a mixing pot

this concoction
will make me forget
the trauma
you sewed into my blood

your punishment
written in ink
laced with glory

to be a year older in new york

on the way to brooklyn
the train does its smooth dance
& i smile

my throat is jagged
from all our memories getting caught
on my oesophagus

this weekend
it's winter birthday crowns
fluffy pink clueless heels
    that i'll remember   forever

love bites on shoulders
urgent puffer jackets
because it's so fucking freezing

i feel peculiar
not old not young
not full of love
but capability

and us girls sit there
in williamsburg,
legs sprawled on gin-soaked floor

hazy and full of pizza
talking about tomorrow
and the boys who left us

kiss me   graffitied on the walls
plants that are pestering to be watered
odd-one-out furniture

the saturday sun sits cross legged
      through the loft windows

penny for your sight

the longing used to reach my gut

a horrible elastic
snapping heart
beating me awake

in the half-noir
i would swallow down days
in hope of a Happening thing

only sometimes would i recognise
the ever changing trees
or that my coffee was lukewarm

and new york handed me a pair of glasses
nature love   warm hand
spectacles
and i cried
inside my organs
because
i could finally see
the details of

east village apartments
clouds lounging about sky
the mist that surrounded my
friends when we talked
about everything that was
happening to us
together.

acknowledgments

i am beyond fortunate to have these vivacious & intelligent people who helped me through the process of this book. thank you to Grant Mower. i owe you everything. thank you for seeing this project through. you saw the vision. special thanks to my mother, Sonja Yelich, who believed in my writing. thank you for supplying me with endless literature growing up.

to Ella, who changed my life. i am so proud to be your sister.

thank you to Robert Mickelson, my incredible agent at CAA. you taught me how to believe in myself.

to my family, for their support of my insane dreams. especially to my dad, who let me move overseas to pursue them.

to my favourite academics, Nicky Woodward & Christopher Lee. for nurturing my skills.

thank you to my wonderful friends. there are too many to list. special thanks to Desiree Brady, Sophie Vincent, Livy Wicks, Caitlin Davidson, Ryan Quint, Jaimee-lee Tredray, Anna-Hall Taylor.

for being my lights, keeping me sane, and loving me unconditionally.

thank you to Savannah Brown, who put up with all my questions.

thank you to Will Tee Yang, for taking the image that inspired this whole book. and Sophia Doak, for shooting the wonderful cover photo. special thanks to Greta Markurt for drawing the beautiful image on the back cover.

and to my icons: Jack Gilbert, Lou Reed, Frank O'Hara,
Charles Bukowski, Patti Smith, Justin Vernon, Whitney
Houston, Cat Stevens, Cyndi Lauper, James Taylor.

finally, to myself. thank you for every reminder, every
sticky note, every notebook. for giving yourself
 the breathing space. for pursuing.

about the author

indy yelich is an 18 year old poet from auckland, new zealand. she is the daughter of renowned kiwi poet, sonja yelich, and younger sister of pop artist, lorde. she currently splits her time between new york, los angeles, and auckland, and has an unhealthy obsession with m&ms and writing herself constant sticky note reminders. *sticky notes* is her first book of poetry.

instagram: @indyyelich1
twitter: @IndyYelich

www.indyyelich.com

CPSIA information can be obtained
at www.ICGtesting.com
Printed in the USA
BVHW092248280922
648181BV00008B/226

9 781388 639075